Meet the Octopus

Eight arms reach out from the shadows of a coral reef. In a flash of color, what looked like a rock suddenly transforms into a graceful, flowing creature. Welcome to the amazing world of the octopus—one of the ocean's most intelligent and mysterious animals!

Octopuses are **marine mollusks** that live in oceans around the world. From shallow tide pools to the deepest ocean trenches, these remarkable creatures have adapted to nearly every marine environment on Earth. You can find them hiding in coral reefs, gliding over sandy ocean floors, and even dwelling in the crushing depths where sunlight never reaches.

Octopus vs Squid

Octopus:
- Soft, round body with no fins
- Has 8 arms, all the same length
- Crawls and squirts water to move
- Lives alone in dens on the ocean floor

Squid:
- Long, torpedo-shaped body with fins
- Has 8 arms plus 2 longer tentacles
- Fast swimmer using jet power and fins
- Swims in open water, often in groups

The octopus belongs to a group of animals called **cephalopod**s, which means "head-foot." This family also includes squid, cuttlefish, and nautiluses. What makes cephalopods special is their incredible intelligence—and octopuses are the smartest of them all.

There are over 300 species of octopus, ranging from the tiny Wolfi octopus, which is smaller than a grape, to the massive Pacific giant octopus, whose arms can span over 30 feet (9 meters) across. Each species has evolved unique abilities and characteristics that help them survive in their underwater world.

These animals are truly alien-like in their abilities. They can change color and texture instantly, squeeze through impossibly small spaces, solve complex puzzles, and even use tools. Once thought to be simple creatures, scientists now know that octopuses are among the most intelligent invertebrates on Earth.

But octopuses face many challenges in today's oceans. From climate change to pollution, these fascinating creatures need our help to survive and thrive for future generations to discover and admire.

What Do Octopuses Look Like?

Octopuses have one of the most unique body designs in the animal kingdom. Their soft, boneless bodies can seem almost magical in how they move and change.

An octopus's body consists of three main parts: the head, the mantle (body), and eight flexible arms. The head contains the brain and eyes, while the mantle houses most of the internal organs. The eight arms, each lined with powerful suction cups, extend from around the mouth.

DID YOU KNOW?
An octopus's suction cups are so sensitive they can tell the difference between different textures, temperatures, and even chemical compositions just by touching them. Each arm has about 300 suction cups, giving them around 2,400 individual "taste buds" on their arms!

Most octopuses have large, complex eyes that are surprisingly similar to human eyes. These eyes can focus, form sharp images, and detect the polarization of light—something humans can't do. Their excellent vision helps them hunt and spot predators in the ocean's dim light.

Each arm is incredibly flexible and strong, covered with hundreds of suction cups that can taste and smell whatever they touch. These arms can move independently—an octopus can search for food with one arm while using another to build a shelter, all without looking.

Perhaps most amazing of all is their skin. Octopuses have specialized cells called chromatophores that contain different colored pigments. By expanding or contracting these cells, they can change color in a fraction of a second. They also have cells that can change the texture of their skin, making it smooth, bumpy, or spiky to match their surroundings.

Unlike most mollusks, octopuses have no external shell. Instead, they have a small internal structure called a pen or gladius that provides some support to their soft bodies. Their only hard part is a sharp, parrot-like beak hidden at the center of their arms.

Blue-Ringed Octopus

Mimic Octopus

Pacific Giant Octopus

Common Octopus

Types of Octopus

With over 300 species around the world, octopuses come in all shapes, sizes, and talents!

Pacific Giant Octopus is the heavyweight champion of the octopus world! It can weigh up to 600 pounds (270 kg) and stretch over 30 feet (9 m). They live in cold northern oceans and are known for their intelligence and problem-solving abilities. Despite their massive size, they can squeeze through any opening larger than their baseball-sized beak.

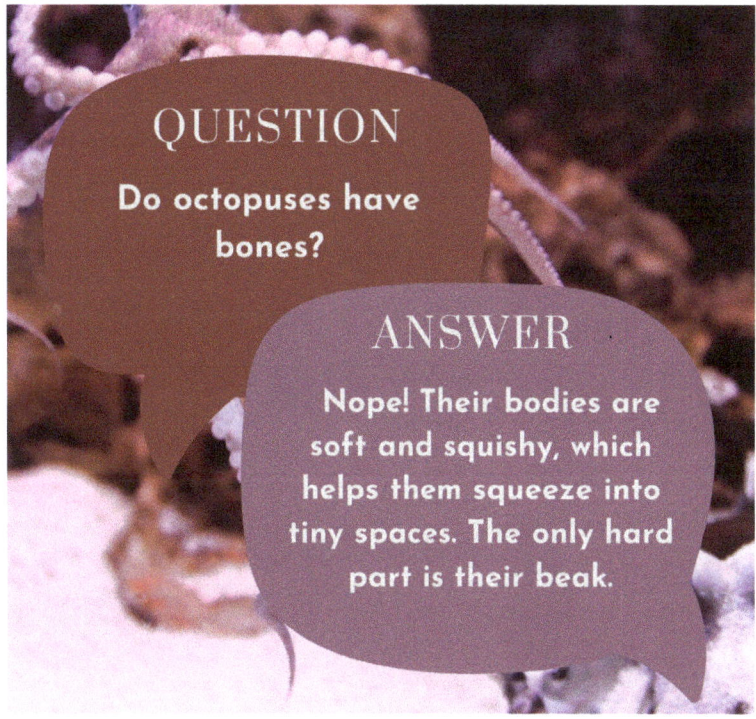

QUESTION
Do octopuses have bones?

ANSWER
Nope! Their bodies are soft and squishy, which helps them squeeze into tiny spaces. The only hard part is their beak.

Blue-Ringed Octopus are tiny but powerful! This golf-ball-sized octopus flashes bright blue rings when it feels threatened. Its venom is dangerous to humans—but it's shy and rarely seen.

Mimic Octopus is the master of disguise. Found in Indonesian waters, it can imitate at least 15 different animals, including flatfish, lionfish, stingrays, and sea snakes. They don't just change color—they actually change their body shape and movement to perfectly copy other creatures.

Dumbo Octopus lives in the deepest parts of the ocean, over 13,000 feet (4,000 meters) down. Named for their ear-like fins that resemble Disney's flying elephant, these adorable creatures glide gracefully through the deep sea. They're about the size of a small dog and feed on tiny creatures that float in the deep ocean.

Common Octopus is probably the species most people think of when they picture an octopus. Found in warm waters around the world, they're excellent problem-solvers and the species most often studied by scientists. They typically weigh 6-22 pounds (3-10 kg) and live in coastal waters.

Wolfi Octopus holds the record as the world's smallest octopus. An adult is smaller than a grape, weighing less than a paperclip. Despite their tiny size, they have all the same abilities as their giant cousins, including color-changing and problem-solving skills.

Each species shows us different ways that evolution has shaped octopuses to survive in specific ocean environments, from frigid polar seas to tropical coral reefs.

Where Do Octopuses Live

From shallow tide pools to the deepest ocean trenches, octopuses have adapted to every ocean zone on Earth.

- **Intertidal Zone (0–40 ft / 0–12 m)**
  These octopuses brave the surf and sun. At low tide, they hide in rock crevices and hold their breath until the water returns.

- **Neritic Zone (40–650 ft / 12–200 m)**
  Coral reefs, kelp forests, and rocky shores—this busy zone is home to the common octopus. With many predators nearby, camouflage is key to survival.

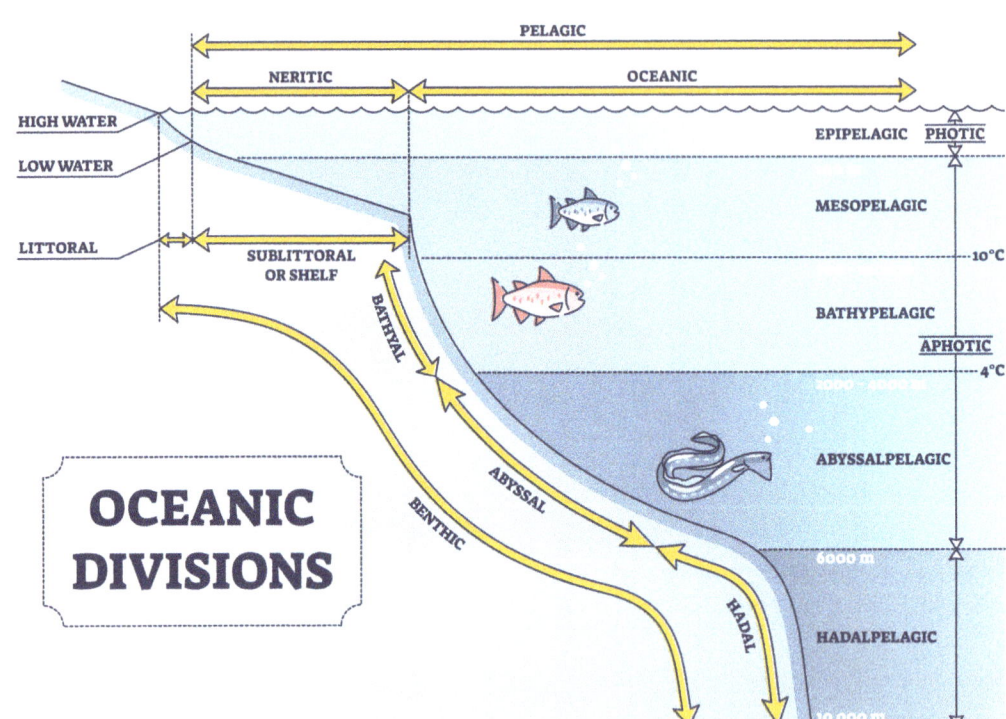

- **Bathyal Zone (650–13,000 ft / 200–4,000 m)**
  Also called the "twilight zone." Light fades, pressure builds, and octopuses here grow larger and slower, with big eyes to spot the faintest glow.

- **Abyssal Zone (13,000–20,000 ft / 4,000–6,000 m)**
  Total darkness. Freezing cold. Crushing pressure. This is home to the dumbo octopus, which glides silently through the deep.

- **Hadal Zone (20,000+ ft / 6,000+ m)**
  The deepest trenches on Earth. Some octopuses live here in near-total mystery—scientists are still discovering how they survive.

Super Survivors – Octopus Adaptations

Octopuses are built for survival. From escaping predators to vanishing in plain sight, they've evolved some of the strangest—and smartest—tools in the ocean.

- **Camouflage Experts:** Octopuses can change their skin color and texture in less than a second to blend into coral, rocks, or sand. Special color cells called chromatophores help them disappear—or flash warning colors when threatened. Some even make their skin bumpy or spiky to match rough surfaces.

- **Jet-Powered Escape:** To escape danger, an octopus fills its body with water and shoots it out through a tube called a siphon, blasting backward like a jet. Many species also release a cloud of dark ink to confuse predators while they make their getaway.

- **No Bones, No Problem:** With no bones, octopuses can squeeze through any opening larger than their beak—the only hard part of their body. Even a giant octopus can slip through a hole the size of a quarter.

MYTH vs FACT

Myth: Octopus ink is just for hiding.

Fact: The ink also contains chemicals that can block a predator's sense of smell and taste—buying the octopus time to escape.

- **Arms That Taste:** Each arm is lined with suction cups that can taste and smell whatever they touch. This helps octopuses find food and sense danger—even in total darkness.

- **Blue Blood & Three Hearts:** Octopuses have three hearts and blue blood. The blue color comes from a copper-based chemical that works better than iron in cold, low-oxygen water. Two hearts pump blood to the gills; the third pumps it to the rest of the body.

Smart as a Whip: Octopus Intelligence

Octopuses are some of the most intelligent animals in the ocean—and possibly the smartest invertebrates on Earth. What makes their brainpower especially fascinating is that it evolved completely separately from the kind of intelligence we see in mammals, birds, or humans.

Problem Solvers and Escape Artists
In experiments, octopuses have solved puzzles, navigated mazes, and even opened childproof containers. They can learn by trial and error, and remember solutions for weeks. One famous octopus named Inky escaped from the National Aquarium of New Zealand. He slipped through a small gap in the top of his tank, crawled across the floor, and disappeared down a drainpipe that led to the sea. It looked like a carefully planned escape.

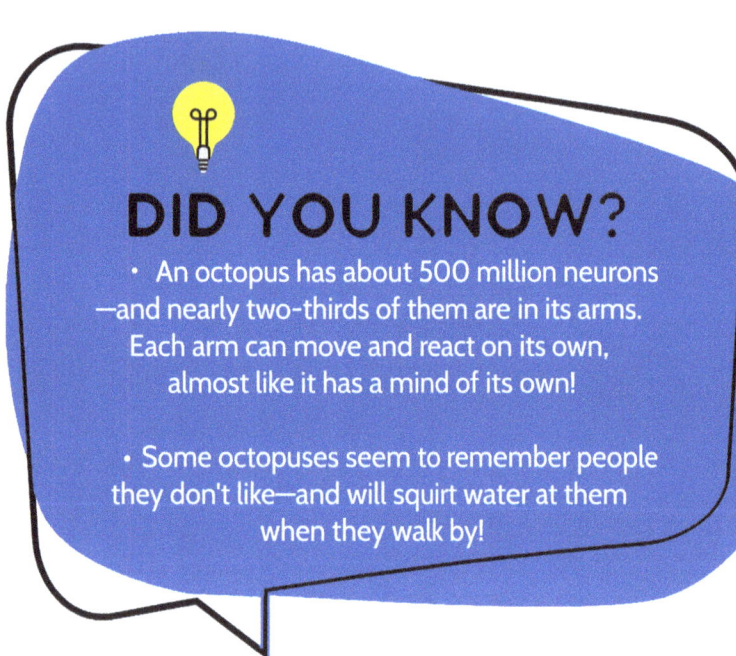

DID YOU KNOW?
- An octopus has about 500 million neurons—and nearly two-thirds of them are in its arms. Each arm can move and react on its own, almost like it has a mind of its own!
- Some octopuses seem to remember people they don't like—and will squirt water at them when they walk by!

Tools, Personalities, and Memory
In the wild, octopuses have been seen collecting coconut shells and stacking them to make shelters. Some use rocks to smash open clams or throw shells at intruders. Each octopus seems to have its own personality—some are shy and cautious, others bold and curious. Aquarium workers say octopuses can recognize individual people and often behave differently depending on who's nearby. There are even reports of octopuses squirting water at people they seem to dislike!

A Brain in Every Arm
An octopus's brain isn't just in its head. About two-thirds of its neurons—the cells that carry messages—are found in its arms. That means each arm can move, react, and even solve simple problems on its own, almost like it's thinking independently. This helps octopuses multitask—exploring a hiding place, reaching for food, and watching for danger all at once.

Silent Signals
Even though octopuses don't make sounds, they're excellent at sending signals. They flash colors, shift textures, and change body shapes to communicate with other animals—or to blend in with their surroundings.

What Do Octopuses Eat?

Octopuses are meat-eaters with serious hunting skills. They'll eat just about anything they can catch—crabs, shrimp, snails, fish, and sometimes even other octopuses. What they eat depends on their size and where they live.

A small octopus might use its arms to poke into cracks and pull out a hiding crab. A giant Pacific octopus, on the other hand, has been seen taking on much larger prey—like fish, lobsters, and even small sharks. These powerful predators grab with their arms, bite with their beak, and inject venom that helps them subdue their catch.

Hidden at the center of their arms is a sharp, parrot-like beak that can crush shells with ease. The beak tears prey into pieces, while the venom starts to break the food down before the octopus even swallows. They don't chew—they tear, digest, and eat it all from the safety of their den.

Quick Facts

- The beak is the only hard part of an octopus's body. It's made of keratin, like your fingernails.
- Some octopuses use rocks as tools to smash open shells—something only a few animals in the world can do!
- Their venom starts digesting prey before they even swallow it—like a built-in stomach in their bite.
- Octopuses are opportunistic carnivores—they'll hunt almost anything that moves, as long as they can catch it.
- They "taste" with their arms! Each suction cup has special sensors that help them detect food by touch.

Octopuses are primarily ambush predators. They typically hunt by hiding in their dens and waiting for prey to come close, then striking with lightning speed. Their arms can shoot out and grab prey in milliseconds. Some species also actively hunt by walking along the ocean floor, using their arms to flip over rocks and search for hidden creatures.

They have excellent vision that helps them spot prey from a distance. In darker waters, they rely more on their sense of touch and chemical detection through their suction cups. Some species have even been seen using tools—like stacking shells to hide behind while stalking prey or smashing clams open with rocks.

Their eyesight is excellent, and their suction cups can "taste" what they touch—so even in the dark, they're hard to fool. Once an octopus catches its meal, very little goes to waste.

Do Octopuses Have a Social Life?

Adult octopuses usually settle near a den and claim a patch of ocean floor. Some guard just a few square yards, while others roam over much larger areas. If another octopus comes too close, the message is often clear: This space is taken. Instead of fighting, they usually flash warning colors or retreat—serious battles are rare.

Octopuses don't make sounds, but they communicate in silent but striking ways. They change their skin color and texture to send signals. Stripes or dark patterns often mean "stay away," while pale shades might show fear or stress. Some species even perform a "passing cloud" display, where waves of dark color roll across their bodies like moving shadows.

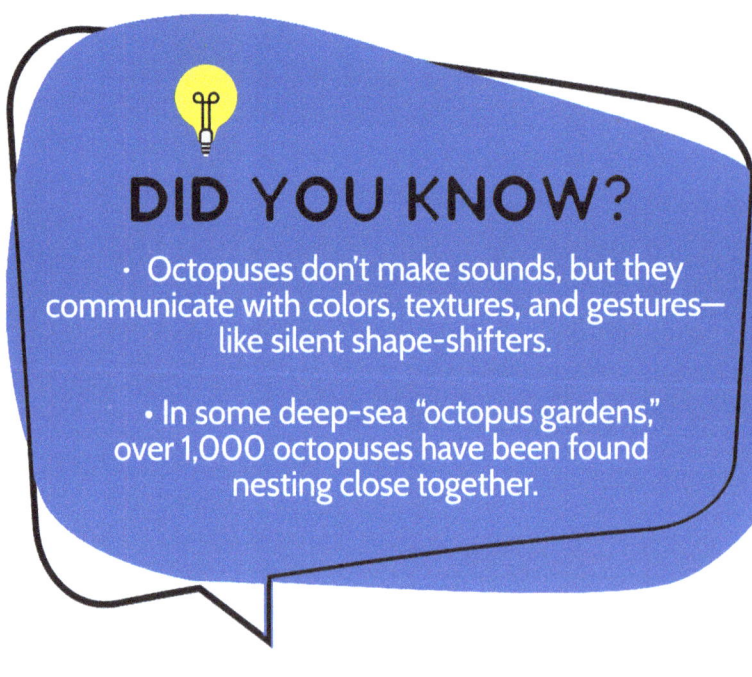

DID YOU KNOW?

- Octopuses don't make sounds, but they communicate with colors, textures, and gestures—like silent shape-shifters.

- In some deep-sea "octopus gardens," over 1,000 octopuses have been found nesting close together.

Body language matters, too. An octopus might raise its arms to look bigger, spread out across the seafloor, or make twisting motions with its limbs. Scientists think some of these movements may be like gestures—or even a kind of sign language.

Even in aquariums, octopuses quickly show they notice who's who. Some are friendly with certain caretakers and splash water at people they dislike. In fact, they've been known to squirt at visitors they find annoying—and some even aim well enough to knock objects off tables.

They're also particular about their homes. Many octopuses keep their dens neat, pushing out sand and piling up shells. Some arrange bits of bone, rock, or trash outside—almost like decoration or a warning sign to others.

Although they mostly live alone, octopuses are still curious. Scientists have seen them cautiously interacting in the wild—brief touches, arm signals, or color changes that show interest instead of aggression. These encounters are rare, but they suggest octopuses are more socially aware than we once believed.

On the Move

Octopuses have developed several unusual ways to travel through the ocean—whether they're hunting, exploring, or escaping danger.

Most of the time, they crawl along the seafloor using their arms. This movement, sometimes called "walking," is more like flowing across the ground. They use their suction cups to grip rocks, coral, and sand as they pull themselves forward. It's slow but efficient—and helps them stay hidden from predators and prey alike.

When they need to escape fast, octopuses switch to jet propulsion. They suck water into their body and blast it out through a tube called a siphon, shooting backward at high speed. This can launch them up to 25 miles per hour (40 km/h), but it takes a lot of energy—so they use it only for quick getaways.

Some species swim by gently waving their arms in a graceful motion. Others, like the deep-sea dumbo octopus, use ear-like fins to glide through the water in near silence. These methods are better for open water or deep habitats where crawling isn't practical.

Octopuses can even move on land—for short periods. Some tide pool species leave the water during low tide to crawl across wet rocks and hunt in nearby pools. They can't stay out long, though, or they risk drying out.

Different species have different movement habits. Some stay close to their dens and make short foraging trips, while deep-sea species may drift longer distances, following food or changes in temperature. Whether creeping or blasting away, octopuses are always adapting their movement to fit their environment.

A Day in the Life

Octopuses are nocturnal animals, which means they're most active at night. When the sun goes down, they leave their dens and begin their nightly routine—hunting, exploring, and staying alert for danger.

An octopus's den might be a pile of rocks, a coral crevice, or even an old shell. Some octopuses decorate the entrance with bits of shell, bone, or debris—both to stay hidden and to warn them if something disturbs their home while they're away.

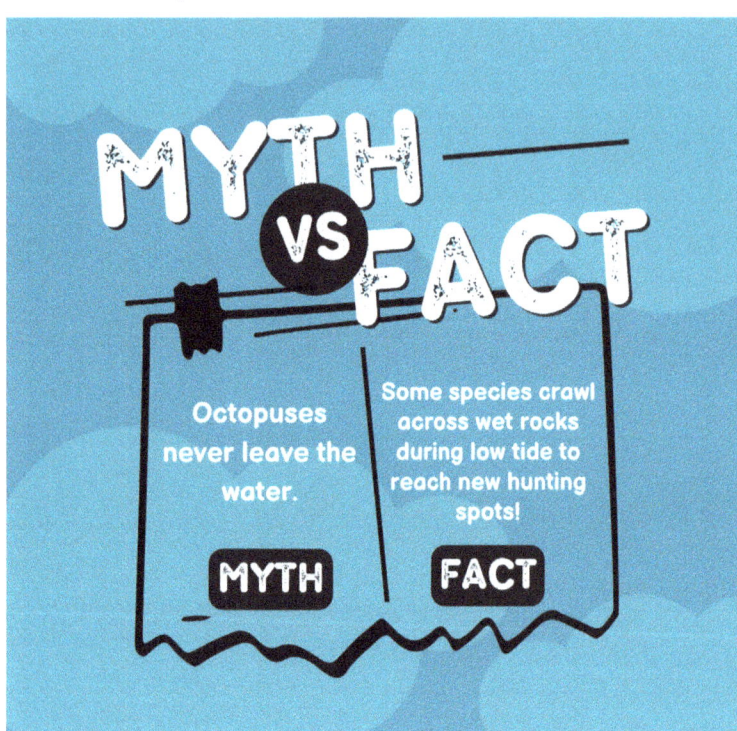

Hunting is usually the first task of the night. Octopuses have excellent night vision, and they use their arms to feel into cracks and crevices, searching for crabs, shrimp, and other small creatures. Their suction cups can even "taste" what they touch. When prey is found, the attack is fast. One arm—or several—shoots out to grab it, and the octopus delivers a venomous bite with its beak to stop the struggle.

After feeding, most octopuses return to their dens to rest and digest. They don't sleep like mammals, but they do have quiet periods during the day. Scientists believe octopuses experience a form of dream-like sleep. While resting, their skin sometimes shifts colors and patterns—almost as if they're reliving moments or imagining new ones.

Octopuses also spend time maintaining their dens. They move rocks, sweep out sand, and sometimes rearrange or "decorate" with interesting objects. Some even seem to prefer certain shapes or colors, hinting at individual personalities.

Even during rest, they remain watchful. Their sharp eyes scan for predators, and their skin can change color in an instant—helping them vanish into the background if danger appears.

For a solitary animal, the octopus leads a surprisingly busy life—full of clever hunting, quiet observation, and constant adjustment to the ever-changing world of the sea.

Mating and Birth

For most octopuses, reproduction is a once-in-a-lifetime event. After mating, both the male and female die—making the next generation their final mission.

When mating season begins, male octopuses face a dangerous challenge: getting close to a female without being eaten. Females are often larger and may mistake an approaching male for prey. To avoid this, males use a mix of caution and creativity. Some approach slowly, while others flash colors and move their arms in specific patterns—almost like a dance.

Mating involves a special arm called the hectocotylus, which the male uses to transfer sperm to the female. In some species, this arm actually breaks off and stays with the female. This strange strategy helps ensure success—while the male swims away and lives a little longer (but usually not much).

After mating, the female finds a safe place to lay her eggs. Depending on the species, she might lay just a few dozen—or over 100,000. The eggs are small and pearl-like, often hanging from the roof of a den in long strings.

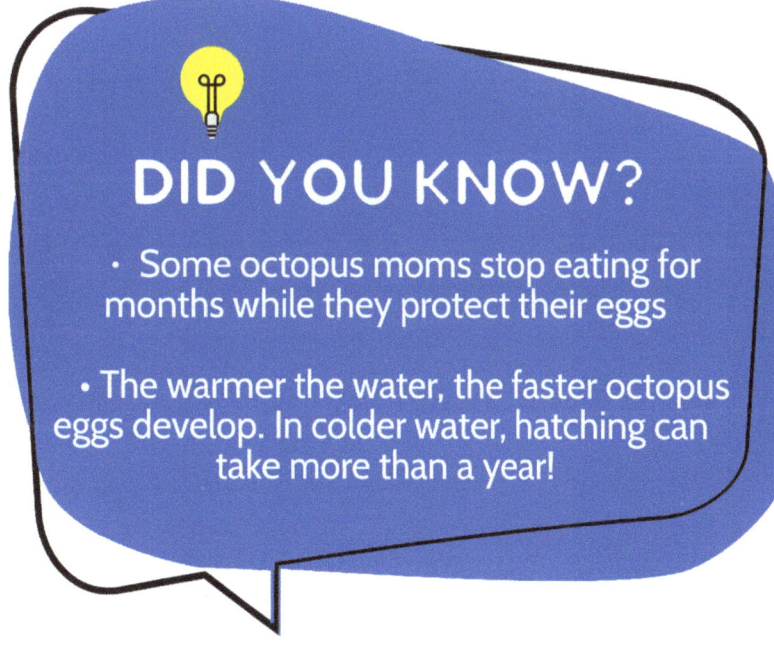

DID YOU KNOW?

- Some octopus moms stop eating for months while they protect their eggs

- The warmer the water, the faster octopus eggs develop. In colder water, hatching can take more than a year!

From that moment on, her life revolves around protecting them. She guards the eggs constantly, gently fanning them with her arms to keep water flowing and cleaning off sand or algae. Most females stop eating entirely during this time. She stays in her den for weeks or even months, growing weaker while the babies develop.

When the eggs finally hatch, the mother's job is done. She usually dies shortly afterward, having devoted all her energy to giving the next generation a strong start.

The exact timing of hatching depends on the water temperature. Warmer water speeds up development; colder water slows it down. This helps the babies hatch when food will be most available—a clever trick built into nature itself.

Growing Up Octopus

The moment a baby octopus hatches, it begins life alone. Its mother is gone, and it must face the world without help. But even at the size of a grain of rice, it already has everything it needs—eight tiny arms, the ability to change color, and jet-powered movement.

Some species hatch as free-floating babies, drifting in the open ocean like specks of living dust. These tiny explorers are part of the plankton community, carried by currents and feeding on microscopic creatures. Others skip the drifting stage and settle straight to the sea floor, crawling into cracks and crevices like miniature adults.

No matter how they start, young octopuses face enormous danger. In the open ocean, almost everything is a predator—fish, jellyfish, even other octopus. Scientists estimate that fewer than 1 in 100 baby octopuses survives to adulthood.

Growing Up Timeline

DAY 1 - HATCHLING
Baby octopuses hatch fully formed but tiny—some about the size of a grain of rice—and begin life on their own.

DAY 1 TO ~30–60 DAYS
Some babies float in the open ocean as plankton; others settle to the seafloor right away. Survival rates are very low.

1-4 MONTHS
Young octopuses grow fast, practice hunting, build dens, and learn how to survive.

4-8 MONTHS
Young Adult; they hunt larger prey, refine their camouflage, and patrol a home area.

8 MONTHS-2+ YEARS
Now fully grown, octopuses live alone and prepare to reproduce—starting the cycle again.

Those that make it grow at incredible speeds. A baby octopus can multiply its weight by thousands of times in just a few months. To do that, it must eat constantly—hunting tiny shrimp, crabs, and worms, and learning through trial and error how to catch them.

They also practice hiding. Even at a young age, octopuses know how to use camouflage, fit into tight spaces, and build simple dens. While their instincts give them a strong start, each young octopus learns from experience—figuring out how to hunt, where to hide, and when to run.

Growing up as an octopus means growing fast, staying hidden, and adapting to a dangerous world. For the few that survive, it's a remarkable journey from invisible hatchling to one of the ocean's most skilled predators.

Octopuses and Their Ecosystem

Octopuses aren't just clever hunters—they're key players in the ocean's food web. From controlling crab populations to creating shelter for smaller animals, these solitary creatures have a big impact on marine life.

As predators, octopuses help keep the ocean balanced. They hunt crabs, shrimp, and fish, preventing any one species from taking over coral reefs or kelp forests. Without predators like octopuses, some animals could crowd out others and damage the ecosystem.

At the same time, octopuses are food for many larger animals—like sharks, seals, dolphins, and even seabirds. Even their eggs feed smaller creatures if the mother can't defend them. They're an important link between different levels of the food chain.

Octopuses also shape the ocean floor. When they build dens, they rearrange rocks, dig small pits, and pile up shells. These leftover shelters often become homes for other animals like crabs, worms, or small fish. In a way, they act like tiny architects—designing hideouts for ocean life.

By moving through different parts of the seafloor, they also spread nutrients. Their waste adds fertilizer to the water, which helps support tiny organisms and plants. Even when an octopus dies, its body becomes food for scavengers and helps recycle nutrients back into the ecosystem.

Octopuses are also indicator species, which means their presence can tell scientists how healthy the ocean is. If octopus numbers drop, it could be a sign of pollution, overfishing, or rising ocean temperatures.

In short: protect the octopus, and you protect the entire ocean neighborhood.

Predators and Defenses

Even with their incredible brains and camouflage tricks, octopuses have a long list of enemies. Their soft, meaty bodies are a favorite meal for many animals in the sea—and even some above it.

Big fish like groupers, moray eels, and sharks often hunt by ambush, lunging from hidden spots in coral reefs. Marine mammals such as dolphins, seals, and sea otters are skilled hunters, too. Dolphins have been seen tossing octopuses through the water before eating them—possibly to disable them. Sea otters will smash them open using rocks.

From above, seabirds are always watching. In shallow water, diving birds like pelicans and cormorants can spot octopuses from the surface and strike fast. Even tide pools aren't safe.

Surprisingly, other octopuses can be just as dangerous. Larger octopuses sometimes attack and eat smaller ones—especially when food is scarce. Some squid are also known to hunt octopuses, making cephalopods both predator and prey.

But octopuses don't just sit there—they fight back (or slip away). Their defenses are some of the most impressive in the animal kingdom:

- **Camouflage:** Their number one defense. By changing color and texture, octopuses can become nearly invisible in an instant.
- **Ink clouds:** A quick blast of ink confuses predators and may block their sense of smell, giving the octopus time to escape.
- **Arm drop:** If caught, an octopus can detach an arm—which keeps moving to distract the predator while the rest of the octopus slips away. The arm grows back later.
- **Jet escape:** A blast of water from their siphon lets them shoot away quickly, like a rocket.
- **Hidden homes:** A well-built den gives an octopus a safe place to hide—and some dens even have multiple exits for sneaky getaways.

Even with all these tricks, octopuses are always on high alert. Their lives are short and full of danger—but their clever defenses give them a fighting chance.

Challenges and Threats

Life in the ocean has never been easy—but now octopuses face new challenges caused by people. From climate change to plastic pollution, human activity is making it harder for these animals to survive.

Warming oceans are one of the biggest threats. Octopuses don't handle heat well. Warmer water affects how they breathe, how they grow, and even how they find food. Some baby octopuses are hatching too early—before there's enough food around to survive. Acid in the ocean (from pollution in the air) also hurts the shells of crabs and clams—important prey for many octopus species.

Pollution is everywhere. Octopuses are curious and often touch or taste things with their arms, including plastic. A bottle cap or food wrapper might be mistaken for food. Swallowing plastic can block their insides or poison them. Chemicals like oil, pesticides, and heavy metals can build up in the water, and in the bodies of sea creatures.

Overfishing causes trouble too. In some places, people catch too many octopuses, which lowers their numbers. In other areas, fishers take too many of the animals octopuses eat—like shrimp or small fish—leaving them with less food and poorer health.

How You Can Help Octopus

- **Skip the single-use plastic.** Say no to straws, bags, and wrappers that might end up in the ocean.
- ♻ **Recycle and reuse.** Keep trash out of the water by sorting waste and using items more than once.
- 🐟 **Choose ocean-friendly seafood.** If your family eats seafood, look for sustainable options (check for a blue MSC label).
- 🌱 **Support clean oceans.** Join a beach or park cleanup—or help keep your neighborhood litter-free. It all flows downstream!
- 🔊 **Protect ocean quiet.** Turn down boat or watercraft noise when possible, and talk to adults about quieter ocean choices.

Habitat loss is another growing problem. Coastal building projects can wipe out tide pools and shallow reefs. Deep-sea mining damages ocean floor habitats. Coral reefs are also disappearing—taking shelter and hunting grounds with them.

Noise pollution in the ocean is rising, too. Ships, sonar, and underwater construction make it harder for marine animals to navigate, rest, and interact. Scientists think this may stress octopuses and interfere with their behavior.

Invasive species—animals that don't belong in a certain area—can also cause problems. Some compete with octopuses for food. Others may eat young octopuses that haven't evolved ways to escape.

Hope for the Future. There's still time to help. Marine protected areas, better fishing rules, cleaner energy, and international cooperation are all part of the solution. When we take care of the ocean, we help creatures like the octopus—and ourselves.

Short Lives, Big Impact

Octopuses don't live very long. Most species survive only one to five years—even the smartest and largest ones. Their short lifespan is part of what makes them so fascinating. After they reproduce, their story usually ends.

Tiny octopuses like the Wolfi may live just six months. Common octopuses last about a year and a half. The giant Pacific octopus lives the longest—up to five years in cold, deep waters where everything moves slowly, including time.

Temperature plays a big role. In warm water, octopuses grow fast and die young. In cold water, they grow more slowly and live longer. That's why deep-sea and Arctic species often have longer lives than tropical ones.

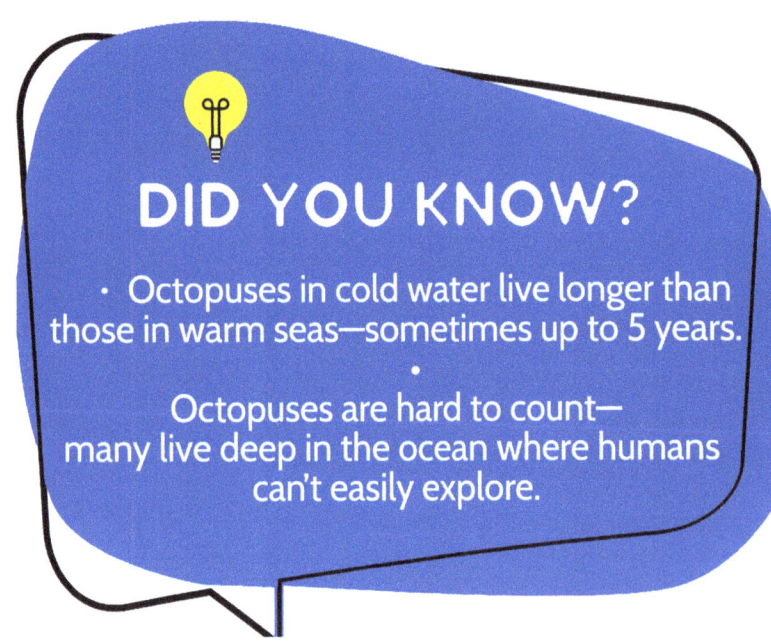

DID YOU KNOW?

- Octopuses in cold water live longer than those in warm seas—sometimes up to 5 years.
- Octopuses are hard to count—many live deep in the ocean where humans can't easily explore.

But tracking octopus populations is tricky. They're experts at hiding, and many live in hard-to-reach places like deep ocean canyons. Scientists have identified more than 300 octopus species so far, but new ones are still being discovered.

Some octopus populations are doing well, especially in shallow coastal areas. Others are under pressure from overfishing and habitat destruction. In the Mediterranean, for example, the common octopus has declined in some regions where it's caught too often.

The deep sea holds even more mysteries. Recent discoveries—like massive "octopus gardens" where females gather to lay their eggs—show how much we still have to learn. These habitats may be threatened by deep-sea mining and climate change, but we don't yet know the full impact.

Because octopuses live short lives and have no time to recover from bad years, they're especially vulnerable to changes in their environment. If water gets too warm, food becomes scarce, or young octopuses can't survive, entire populations could drop quickly.

Most octopus species aren't endangered right now—but that doesn't mean they're safe. Scientists are calling for better tracking, smarter fishing rules, and more protected areas where octopuses can live and reproduce without human disturbance.

Throughout this book, we've explored what makes octopuses some of the most surprising animals in the ocean. They can squeeze through tiny cracks, vanish in plain sight, and even solve problems like a puzzle master. No bones, no shell—just brains, arms, and incredible skill.

They live in coral reefs, tide pools, kelp forests, and deep-sea canyons all over the world. Some are no bigger than a grape. Others are as wide as a car. No matter their size, octopuses help keep the ocean in balance—hunting, hiding, and building homes that other animals use long after they're gone.

But like many ocean creatures, octopuses face growing challenges. Pollution, climate change, overfishing, and habitat loss make it harder for them to survive. The good news? People around the world are working to protect them—and you can be part of that, too.

Octopuses remind us how strange, smart, and beautiful ocean life can be. By learning about them, we learn how to take better care of the sea—and all the amazing animals that call it home.

Word Search

```
Y R A T I L O S S X D K A E B
E V H D S K L U B F T S U R A
E C F U T K P G Z L N K X G D
N P O F N O C Y F T E S G C E
L Q E S T T S G N A G U E A F
A J Y C Y E I K Y T I L G M E
L D O I I S Q N L I L L G O N
F U A C T N T A G B L O S U S
P X E P B P N E K A E M X F E
A P A B T R W N M H T E L L S
S K V H U A I T I X N W D A U
U E O T P Q T P O K I Z H G M
D Y C C H C Y I B W D B G E D
N O C E P H A L O P O D S T E
N M Y K J P T S F N Y E R P N
B H A T C H I N G T E O G Z S
W S R O T A D E R P W R P Q T
Z D O D O C E A N D V B L P R
```

Adaptation	Eggs	Nocturnal
Beak	Habitat	Ocean
Camouflage	Hatching	Octopus
Cephalopods	Hunting	Predators
Defenses	Ink	Prey
Dens	Intelligent	Solitary
Ecosystem	Mollusks	Species

Resources and References

Anderson, Roland C., and Jennifer A. Mather. *Octopus: The Ocean's Intelligent Invertebrate*. Timber Press, 2010.

DK Find Out! "Octopus Facts." DK Find Out!, www.dkfindout.com/us/animals-and-nature/sea-creatures/octopuses.

Keating, Jess. *Ocean Animals: Who's Who in the Deep Blue*. Knopf Books for Young Readers, 2016.

Monterey Bay Aquarium. "Octopuses and Their Relatives." Monterey Bay Aquarium, www.montereybayaquarium.org/animals/octopus.

National Geographic Kids. "Octopus." National Geographic Kids, kids.nationalgeographic.com/animals/invertebrates/facts/octopus.

NOAA Fisheries. "Octopus Biology and Behavior." NOAA Fisheries, www.fisheries.noaa.gov/species/octopus.

Smithsonian Ocean Portal. "Cephalopods: Octopuses, Squid, and Cuttlefish." Ocean Portal, Smithsonian Institution, ocean.si.edu/ocean-life/invertebrates/cephalopods.

Stewart, Melissa. A Place for Fish. Peachtree Publishing, 2014.

Swinburne, Stephen R. Into the Sea. NorthWord Press, 1992.

Wells, Rosemary. Octopuses. Children's Press, 2001.

Published by Dylanna Press an imprint of Dylanna Publishing, Inc.
Copyright © 2025 by Dylanna Press
Author: Tyler Grady
All rights reserved. No part of this publication may be reproduced, stored in a retrieval system, or transmitted by any means, including electronic, mechanical, photocopying, or otherwise, without prior written permission of the publisher.

Although the publisher has taken all reasonable care in the preparation of this book, we make no warranty about the accuracy or completeness of its content and, to the maximum extent permitted, disclaim all liability arising from its use.

www.ingramcontent.com/pod-product-compliance
Lightning Source LLC
Chambersburg PA
CBHW040224040426
42333CB00051B/3444